DEMO

And How To
Deal With Them

**Volume 2 of the Satan, Demons, and Demon
Possession Series**

By Kenneth E. Hagin

Second Edition
Tenth Printing 1989

ISBN 0-89276-026-5

In the U.S. write:
Kenneth Hagin Ministries
P.O. Box 50126
Tulsa, OK 74150-0126

In Canada write:
Kenneth Hagin Ministries
P.O. Box 335
Islington (Toronto), Ontario
Canada, M9A 4X3

Contents

The Satan, Demons, and Demon Possession Series:

Volume 1 — *The Origin and Operation of Demons*
Volume 2 — *Demons and How To Deal With Them*
Volume 3 — *Ministering to the Oppressed*
Volume 4 — *Bible Answers to Man's Questions on Demons*

Chapter 1
How Demons Indwell Man's Spirit

We established in our first book on demons that the devil and demons (or evil spirits) are fallen beings. Regardless of their previous state, it stands without argument that they fell, and that they seek embodiment in man. The Word of God tells us this in Matthew 12:

> MATTHEW 12:43-45
> 43 When the unclean spirit is gone out of a man, he walketh through dry places, seeking rest, and findeth none.
> 44 Then he saith, I will return into my house from whence I came out; and when he is come, he findeth it empty, swept, and garnished.
> 45 Then goeth he, and taketh with himself seven other spirits more wicked than himself, and they enter in and dwell there . . . .

We also learn about demons seeking embodiment in man in the story of the Gadarene demoniac in Mark 5. The madman of Gadara was possessed with the devil and had a legion of spirits in him.

If demons can't embody man, they'll seek to go into animals as their second choice. When Jesus delivered the demoniac, the evil spirits didn't want Him to send them out of the country, so they asked to go into a herd of swine. Jesus gave them permission.

It's obvious why evil spirits seek embodiment in man. They do it because they need a body in order to find their fullest expression in this physical world. They don't have a physical body, because they're spirits. But a physical body gives them greater freedom to manifest in this realm. They can manifest to a certain extent in the spiritual realm even without a body. They can make themselves heard, felt, and known as they come to oppress. None of us is immune to that, but thank God we can learn to exercise authority over the devil and evil spirits. When a demon does find embodiment in a man, it makes that man what it is.

The Word of God tells us in Mark 5 that when Jesus crossed over the Sea of Galilee to the country of the Gadarenes, a man possessed with an unclean spirit came out of a tomb. He also had a legion of demons. This unclean spirit caused the man to become unclean. It caused him to tear off his clothes, wander around naked, and cut himself with stones. This is an illustration, no doubt, of an evil spirit in connection with the sexual appetite of man. This fellow was a sadist. When an unclean spirit controls a person or embodies him, it makes him unclean. A lying spirit makes a liar out of a person.

In addition to these spirits finding embodiment in man, they sometimes attack people physically. That doesn't mean the person is demon possessed, but it means his body is oppressed by that spirit.

In Acts 10:38 we are told about Peter preaching to Cornelius and his household. Peter said Jesus "...*went about doing good, and healing all that were oppressed of the devil....*" Here Peter is calling sickness and disease satanic oppression. The Word of God tells us that when Jesus was dealing with a blind person, He was dealing with a blind spirit (Matt. 12:22). The spirit caused the man to be blind.

The Word of God also speaks of a deaf spirit. This means the spirit is present and must be dealt with before the person can hear. Notice what happened when Jesus came down from the Mount of Transfiguration.

MARK 9:14-17
14 And when he came to his disciples, he saw a great multitude about them, and the scribes questioning with them.
15 And straightway all the people, when they beheld him, were greatly amazed, and running to him saluted him.

16 And he asked the scribes, What question ye with them?
17 And one of the multitude answered and said, Master,
I have brought unto thee my son, which hath a dumb spirit.

Matthew records that the man said his son was a lunatic. Evidently he had some kind of seizures, perhaps similar to epilepsy, and couldn't talk because of the epilepsy.

The 18th verse continues:

MARK 9:18-27
18 And wheresoever he taketh him, he teareth him: and he foameth, and gnasheth with his teeth, and pineth away: and I spake to thy disciples that they should cast him out; and they could not.
19 He answereth him, and saith, O faithless generation, how long shall I be with you? how long shall I suffer you? bring him unto me.
20 And they brought him unto him: and when he saw him, straightway the spirit tare him; and he fell on the ground, and wallowed foaming.
21 And he asked his father, How long is it ago since this came unto him? And he said, Of a child.
22 And ofttimes it hath cast him into the fire, and into the waters, to destroy him: but if thou canst do any thing, have compassion on us, and help us.
23 Jesus said unto him, If thou canst believe, all things are possible to him that believeth.
24 And straightway the father of the child cried out, and said with tears, Lord, I believe; help thou mine unbelief.
25 When Jesus saw that the people came running together, he rebuked the foul spirit, saying unto him, Thou dumb and deaf spirit, I charge thee, come out of him, and enter no more into him.
26 And the spirit cried, and rent him sore, and came out of him: and he was as one dead; insomuch that many said, He is dead.
27 But Jesus took him by the hand, and lifted him up; and he arose.

What Does "Full Possession" Mean?

When I talk about demon possession, I'm not talking about instances like this. This was a case where the demon was in a person's body. But *when one is fully possessed of the devil, he is possessed spirit, soul, and body.* The body can merely be oppressed and evil spirits can be in the house in which you live (your body) and not actually (in the fullest sense) be in *you.*

I've heard preachers say things that have made me cringe on the inside. They leave the impression that all Christians have demons in them. That isn't true. These people don't divide man correctly. Paul said in First Thessalonians 5:23, *"And the very God of peace sanctify you wholly; and I pray God your whole SPIRIT and SOUL and BODY be preserved blameless unto the coming of our Lord Jesus Christ."*

That Scripture tells us man is spirit, soul, and body. Someone said that man is a tripartite being: part is spirit, part is soul, and part is body. But I don't like to say it that way, because it isn't true. That is misleading. *Man actually is a spirit. He has a soul, and he lives in a body.* When expressed like that, it takes on a different meaning. I can prove my statement.

When man dies physically, he still lives. The Bible says he does. Paul, in Second Corinthians 5:1, says, *"For we know that if our earthly house of this tabernacle were dissolved, we have a building of God, an house not made with hands, eternal in the heavens."* He's talking about the inward man and the outward man here.

Paul also says in Second Corinthians 4:16, *"For which cause we faint not: but though our OUTWARD man perish, yet the INWARD man is renewed day by day."*
Second Corinthians 5:6-8 tells us:

2 CORINTHIANS 5:6-8
6 Therefore we are always confident, knowing that, whilst we are at home in the body, we are absent from the Lord:
7 (For we walk by faith, not by sight:)
8 We are confident, I say, and willing rather to be absent from the body, and to be present with the Lord.

When I'm absent from the body, I'm going to be present with the Lord. Paul, of course, is writing to Christians. He said, in writing to the Church at Philippi:

PHILIPPIANS 1:21-23
21 For to me to live is Christ, and to die is gain. [It's a gain to die a physical death.]
22 But if I live in the flesh, this is the fruit of my labour: yet what I shall choose I wot not.
23 For I am in a strait betwixt two, having a desire to depart, and to be with Christ; which is far better.

He is saying that he is going to depart. He is going to be with Christ. The man on the inside is the real man. He is a spirit man. You are a spirit being. You have a soul that is composed of intellectual and emotional qualities, but you live in a body.

Our spirits are reborn when we're born again. First Peter 3:4 says, *"But let it be the hidden man of the heart . . . ."* Your heart is your spirit. Second Corinthians 5:17 says, *"Therefore if any man be in Christ, he is a new creature: old things are passed away; behold, all things are become new."*

This man being talked about here cannot be the body, because you do not have a new body when you are born again. (Thank God, we will have a new body someday.) It is the man on the inside who is a new man.

This man who is a new creature doesn't have a devil in him. He has the nature of God in him and not the nature of the devil. Wouldn't that be an ugly creature — half-God and half-devil? No, the new man doesn't have the nature of the devil in him anymore. That nature he has to deal with is the fleshly nature. It is his body which has not yet been redeemed. He's going to have to do something about that. God isn't going to do anything about it. The Scripture says, "...*old things are passed away....*" (2 Cor. 5:17). If there were any devils or demons in your spirit, they are gone. That old nature of spiritual death has passed away. All things have become new.

You know just as well as I that things haven't become new with the body when you're born again. You have the same body you had. You have the same inclinations you had. The body is not redeemed. Romans 8 says we're waiting for that. It hasn't happened yet, but it will when Jesus comes again.

With the body and our senses we contact this physical world. Satan is the god of this world. You can readily see, then, that he can have contact with this world. The physical man operates in the world where Satan is god. God is god in the spirit world.

Paul speaks about the prince of the power of the air (Eph. 2:2). Spirits are here trying to get into us. They're trying to work on the physical. The devil is the author of sickness and disease. There wasn't any sickness and disease here before Adam sinned. God had seen that His creation was good (Gen. 1:31).

It was after Satan became god of this world that he began to pollute the air with disease germs so small they couldn't be seen with the natural eye.

Is Satan Always the Cause of Disease?

Dr. John G. Lake traveled to Africa as a missionary at the turn of the century. He originally had been a Methodist minister, but had gotten discouraged. He quit the ministry and went into the insurance business, becoming very successful.

Later, he got back into fellowship with God and received the baptism in the Holy Spirit. He went to Africa, where he preached and established hundreds of churches in five years. While he was there, an outbreak of bubonic plague occurred.

In the book *The John G. Lake Sermons on Dominion Over Demons, Disease and Death,* edited by Gordon Lindsay, Dr. Lake recalled that he and a Dutchman buried many who had died from the plague. They went into the people's homes, carried the bodies out, dug the graves, and buried the dead. "Sometimes we would put three or four in one grave," Lake noted. Yet he and the Dutchman never contracted the disease.

The plague was so severe that the British government sent a shipload of doctors and medical supplies to South Africa to relieve the suffering.

Hearing of Lake's work, one of the doctors sent for him. He asked Lake, "What have you been using to protect yourself? . . .We concluded that if a man could stay on the ground as you have, and keep ministering to the sick and burying the dead, you must have a secret. What is it?"

Lake answered, "Brother, that is the 'law of the Spirit of life in Christ Jesus.' I believe that just as long as I keep my soul in contact with the living God so that His Spirit is flowing into my soul and body, that no germ will ever attach itself to me, for the Spirit of God will kill it."

The doctor suggested that Lake use the same preventatives that the doctors were using as protection from the plague. But Lake, who was deeply interested in science, suggested a scientific experiment instead.

He said, "If you will go over to one of these dead people and take the foam that comes out of their lungs after death, then put it under the microscope, you will see masses of living germs. You will find they are alive until

a reasonable time after a man is dead. You can fill my hand
with them and I will keep it under the microscope, and
instead of these germs remaining alive, they will die
instantly.''

Lake wrote, "They tried it and found it was true."

When they wanted to know how it worked, Lake
explained, "That is 'the law of the Spirit of life in Christ
Jesus.' When a man's spirit and a man's body are filled
with the blessed presence of God, it oozes out of the pores
of your flesh and kills the germs.''

Lake had found the secret. It is knowledge acted upon
that brings results. It doesn't work automatically.

These demons do attack us spiritually, and the devil
is actually behind the thing. Sometimes it is sickness and
disease caused by germs, but the devil is behind it anyhow.
He is an enemy to man and to God. We fight that enemy
with every weapon that is at our disposal.

Sometimes people don't understand why we cast the
devil out of people when we pray for them. One time a
pastor came to me, not understanding why I had done this
to one of his deacons when praying for him. The preacher
thought I was inferring that the deacon was demon
possessed. But I was only indicating he was oppressed.
I hadn't said the demon was in the inward man; it was
in his body. (You might live in a house that has termites
in *it,* but that doesn't mean you have termites in *you.*)

Present Your Body

Paul talks to us about presenting the body as a sacrifice
in Romans 12:

ROMANS 12:1,2
1   I beseech you therefore, brethren, by the mercies of God,
that ye present your bodies a living sacrifice, holy, acceptable unto God, which is your reasonable service.

2 And be not conformed to this world: but be ye transformed by the renewing of your mind, that ye may prove what is that good, and acceptable, and perfect, will of God.

It astounded me when I fully realized what these verses were saying. Paul isn't writing to sinners. He is writing to the saints. He is writing to born-again, Spirit-filled believers. He is telling them even though they are born again, their bodies aren't affected.

So the rebirth is not a physical or mental experience. Being filled with the Spirit is not physical or mental. Both are *spiritual* experiences which eventually affect the physical and mental.

After we're born again and filled with the Holy Spirit, we're to present our bodies to God. He isn't going to do anything about that; it's up to us. If we don't present our bodies to God, and if the inward man isn't in control, then evil spirits will have access. They can dominate us through the flesh.

If we don't get our minds renewed with the Word of God, the MIND will side with the BODY against the SPIRIT. We will be like the Corinthians who were held in a babyhood state of Christianity. They were born again and filled with the Spirit, yet they were carnal. A person can have all the gifts of the Spirit operating in his life and still be carnal.

Carnal Christians can be filled with the Holy Spirit. One woman was asking me about this; she couldn't understand it. I asked her if she were filled with the Holy Spirit, and she said yes. I told her that proved carnal Christians could be filled! Any of us ought to be able to see that. Many times my heart tells me one thing and my head tells me something else. *My heart knows more than my head about spiritual things because I contact the Holy Spirit with my spirit.* But it is hard to get across to my head everything my heart knows.

Sometimes when I preach, people might shudder because they can't understand what is being said. But in your heart it sets up a thrill because your heart knows it's true. Your spirit knows the truth.

Dividing the Soul and Spirit

In my studies it has always been very easy for me to distinguish between the body and the mind. But it becomes a little more difficult when it comes to dividing the soul and spirit. We've never gotten into it like we should. I've read textbooks used in theological seminaries and the way they present this subject is confusing. Only the Word of God can divide:

> **HEBREWS 4:12**
> 12 For the word of God is quick, and powerful, and sharper than any twoedged sword, piercing even to the dividing asunder of soul and spirit, and of the joints and marrow, and is a discerner of the thoughts and intents of the heart.

You can't find in the Bible where the soul and spirit are spoken of as the same thing. I've talked to some great preachers and teachers who say that the soul and the spirit are the same thing, but they can be divided.

That can't be true; they can't be the same thing. In First Thessalonians 5:23 Paul says, *"And the very God of peace sanctify you wholly; and I pray God your whole SPIRIT and SOUL and BODY be preserved blameless unto the coming of our Lord Jesus Christ."* If they're one, why didn't he include them as one?

James wrote to Christians and told them to receive the engrafted word which was able to save their souls (James 1:21). That is the greatest need of the Church today. In John 3:6 Jesus said to Nicodemus, *"That which is born of the flesh is flesh; and that which is born of the Spirit is spirit. "* The New Birth is a spiritual birth. But the body and the soul still have to be dealt with. *You* do that. Paul said we should be transformed by the renewing of our minds.

We have read Psalm 23:3 many times: *"He restoreth my soul. "* The Hebrew word for "restore" and the Greek word for "renew" mean identically the same thing. You can restore a piece of furniture to its original condition. We have to restore or renew our emotional realm. We do it with the Word of God.

Our spirits, however, are reborn. I'll never believe that a born-again Christian *walking in fellowship with God* has a demon in his spirit. You can't find any Scripture to convince me of it. I do know that sometimes in the case of physical sickness there is a spirit that has to be dealt with in the body.

In 1956, I was holding a meeting in a Full Gospel church in Portland, Oregon. On the last night of the meeting there was an unusual occurrence. I prayed for three small children who all were troubled with epileptic seizures.

Both the mother and father were saved. When I laid my hands on the first child, I knew a spirit was causing the seizures. Sometimes sickness can be just a physical thing, but I knew this time it was a spirit. (I do believe, though, that the devil is always behind it.) So I cast that spirit out. When I laid hands on the second child, I had the same manifestation; I cast that spirit out. When I laid hands on the third child, I had the same manifestation again, and cast the spirit out.

The next year when we were in Vancouver, Washington, the parents came to visit our meeting and told us the children never had had another seizure. The youngsters hadn't been demon possessed; they had merely allowed this spirit to get into their bodies. Others have allowed demons into their souls.

Demons in the Emotional Realm

You know my testimony of how I was raised up from the bed of sickness. My mother used to tell me she wished she could take my place. But her own life had been a tragedy. Demons of worry, depression, and oppression got into her emotional or soulish realm and captivated her.

My daddy had left when I was about 5 or 6, leaving her with four little children to raise. He had come from a good family. In fact, my grandfather had been considered a millionaire before the crash of '29. My daddy, however, had been the only son, and after he got married, he wanted everyone to continue giving things to him. He had been set up in business, but he lost a lot of money.

My mother married him anyway and said if she made her bed hard she would lie on it. She didn't want to go back to her mother, so she tried to make a living for us herself.

All the trouble she had began to affect her mentally and physically, and she began to lose her sight until she became totally blind. A little dog would lead her to work. She worked when she was blind and no one knew it. When it was finally discovered, she had to quit.

The doctors who examined her said they couldn't find anything physically wrong with her that would cause the blindness except a nerve. She eventually had a complete nervous, physical and mental breakdown. But she still wouldn't ask for help.

One time we got real hungry and one of the neighbor children came out of his house eating a peanut butter and cracker sandwich. He broke it in two and gave me half of it. I took a bite and then fainted because of the hunger.

When his mother came out and saw me, she went to my mother's folks and told them how hungry I was. They came and got us and my mother gave up entirely. For several years she had mental problems and would even try to kill herself.

My mother was a Christian, but she didn't know how to believe God and appropriate His promises. It is so sad. Somebody might ask, "If she had killed herself, would she have been saved?" Certainly, yes. She didn't have any remembrance of attempting suicide later. She would have denied it. Those demons of worry and oppression had simply gotten into her emotional realm.

Deliverance for the Insane

Years ago a woman told my wife and me that her sister was an inmate in the Wichita Falls, Texas, asylum. She said she had been believing God that I could minister to the sister. I said I would turn the matter over to my prayer group. We had a little group of women in the church who could pray heaven and earth together! They got answers!

About ten days after we had prayed, the authorities said this woman could come home on furlough. They sent a letter to her family saying she was no longer violent, but that she would always need institutional care. She had been in a padded cell for two years, violently insane. Her general health had deteriorated, and the authorities felt that if the change in environment didn't help her, she probably wouldn't live much longer.

I learned that this woman had been a Full Gospel minister, but when she had gone through menopause she had lost her mind. During that time a demon had gotten into the emotional part of her makeup. She either consciously or unconsciously yielded to that thing. She began to worry and brood and became emotionally upset.

In May 1943, she was brought to our parsonage. We were introduced to her and immediately she began to quote Scriptures. They started running out of her mouth like water. I didn't know what to do. I said anyone who knew Scriptures like that must really know God. Her eyes began to flash and she grabbed her hair and pulled it and said, "No!" She said she couldn't be saved because she had committed the unpardonable sin.

A spirit had gotten into her soul and had made her believe she had committed the unpardonable sin. The sister took hold of her and began to shake her to make her be quiet. We sat down and she never batted an eye.

My wife and I went to get a little red-haired woman from our prayer circle who really knew how to pray. Thank God for people who know how to pray. While we were in the car waiting for her, I began to talk to the Lord about what had happened. I knew the woman merely could be sick. People can be sick in the head just as they can in the stomach. You can pray for them and expect God to heal them.

But I also knew an evil spirit could be the cause. In that case the spirit would have to be discerned and dealt with. I told the Lord that He was going to have to help me. I didn't know what to do. I spent my time praying this way until the woman came out, and then we all went back to our house.

We all started praying, and soon we were praying in the Spirit. The Holy Spirit wanted me to go stand in front of the woman and command the unclean devil to come out of her in the Name of Jesus. After much persuasion I did it. She didn't look any different afterwards; her sister bundled her up and took her home.

That was on a Saturday. On Monday afternoon her sister returned and asked us to pray because the woman had had an attack like she had when she first lost her mind.

She became violent. I told her the devil knew I had spoken the Word of faith and he had to go. I told her he was just tearing her before he left.

In the Bible, after Jesus rebuked an evil spirit in people, the devil would sometimes tear them before he came out. I told her that after he did that she would be all right. Sure enough, that is what happened. When the attack was over, her mind was all right.

Since the woman was only on furlough, she had to go back to the institution. But later she was pronounced well and dismissed. I don't believe that this Full Gospel minister had a devil in her *spirit*. I do believe, though, that at a time in her life when she was nervous and unstable, she yielded to an evil spirit and it got into her *soul* — into the realm of emotion. It took over her mind and worked through her *body*.

Demons in the Body

I saw some things along these same lines while teaching in Forth Worth one time. A woman whom I knew came to me about a problem. She and her husband had pastored a church near me at one time. I knew she needed help before she even came to see me, so I began teaching publicly instead of talking to her personally (I didn't want to embarrass her).

When she came to me she told me how much my teaching had helped her. She said it seemed as though a dark cloud had been lifted. She explained that a black cloud had hung over her head for a long time and she hadn't had anyone to whom she could talk. She said I had removed the cloud, but I told her God had done it. I told her I had taught on this subject for her benefit, since I knew all about her problem because Jesus had told me.

This woman's husband had been a wonderful Christian.

He was sweet, kind, and good. One day at a fellowship meeting where I was speaking I had heard him talking to some other ministers. He was nearing 70 at the time. He had been a pioneer in Pentecost, and he had had the baptism of the Holy Spirit before his denomination was even organized.

For years he never had gone to a doctor. He always had enjoyed good health, but finally he began to have trouble physically. The doctor found out he had high blood pressure. He figured this man wouldn't take any medicine, so he put him on a diet and told him to slow down.

Since the man's wife was also a preacher, the doctor said he should let her do some preaching while he took a leave of absence. He did let her preach a little, but he didn't take a leave. He soon began to feel better and decided he would get back in the harness. When he did, his blood pressure crept up again. So now instead of taking a leave of absence, he decided he would resign. He didn't want to be a burden to his church. (They should have been obligated to him, however, as he had established that church thirty years earlier.)

At this time I was 28 years old, and this man was old enough to be my grandpa. The Lord started talking to me about him, and I knew he was missing God. I knew he shouldn't resign that church, but that afternoon he got up and resigned. He should have stayed there and had an income and let his wife do most of the preaching. He might have lived much longer if he had. But he left with no income and went to live with one of his sons, where he had a stroke.

Later he and his wife moved to Texas and he had another stroke. That was followed by a third stroke, although it didn't kill him (he didn't die until after the fourth stroke).

His wife told me later that she and her daughter had

been with him in the hospital. He was partially paralyzed.
At times he wasn't himself. When she came into the room
he would sometimes say to her, "You old So-and-so," and
with his good leg he would kick her and knock her around.

They would pray and pray. He would pray in tongues
and be all right for a while, but he never did get delivered.
His wife said that after hearing me she knew what she
should have done. In her husband's brain were depleted
brain cells and he couldn't use one arm. *He couldn't oversee
his body, so the devil came to take advantage of him,
operating through his body — not his spirit.* She realized
she should have stood there and commanded the devil to
take his hands off God's property. I assured her he would
have done it.

An Unusual Case

Evil spirits get into some people when they are
children, and even though the person gets born again later,
the spirits are in the soul. These demons that attack in
the physical and soulish realms must be discerned and cast
out.

A preacher told me once about his mother, who was
some 80 years of age and was an old-time saint who had
been filled with the Spirit for years. He said she had had
a stroke and couldn't talk. She could hear but she couldn't
answer. He would ask her a question and tell her to raise
one finger if the answer were "yes" and two fingers if the
answer were "no." She always would raise her fingers, so
he knew she could hear.

When the family would pray she would burst out praying in tongues with them, yet she never would say a word
in English. He asked me why this was. I told him the Holy
Spirit is not in your head but in your spirit, and all her
trouble was in her head. Her vocal chords were just as good
as ever.

When you speak in tongues, you speak out of your spirit. Paul said that his spirit prayed. Deaf and dumb people speak with other tongues when they receive the Holy Spirit, because they speak out of their spirits.

Healing of a Marriage

I was holding a meeting in a certain place, and for three nights in a row a young married woman would stay at the altar, crying pathetically, after everyone was dismissed. She would pray in tongues. I knew it was her spirit crying out for help and deliverance. I asked the Lord to show me how to help this young woman.

Suddenly I had a vision of her when she was 9 years old. I saw her coming home from school one day, and when she came into the house she found her mother in bed with another man. You can understand what that would do to the emotions of a 9 year old.

She was now in her 20s. I saw in the Spirit that her trouble was marital trouble. I saw that she had been married two years but because of this emotional block was unable to consummate the marriage. It was breaking the marriage up.

I went to the pastor and asked him if he knew what was wrong with her. He asked if I did, and I told him I did because the Lord had shown me. He said if I knew what to do, I should go ahead and do it. He had prayed and fasted and talked to both of them, but she was getting ready to leave her husband. He wasn't even a Christian, but she was saved and filled with the Spirit.

I went to the young woman and asked if I could speak to her. She said I could. I asked her if she knew what was wrong with her. Then she asked me if I did, and I told her yes. She asked if the pastor had talked to me and I said no.

I told her about my vision. She thought I was a fortune teller, but I told her what I had experienced was from the Spirit of God. After that, she told me that what I had seen was exactly what had happened. She said she loved her husband but never had been able to be a wife to him. I told her that it was wrong for her mother to be in bed with another man, but that marriage wasn't wrong. After giving her a Scripture and talking to her, I laid hands on her and cast that thing out.

The next year I went back to preach a meeting there and she and her husband had a bouncing baby boy whom they had named after me. The husband was now saved and filled with the Holy Spirit. The home was together.

I don't believe that woman had anything in her spirit. But this thing that had gotten into her emotional realm or soul when she was 9 years old still dominated her and had to be dealt with.

Now can you understand why we have problems in our churches? We sometimes act as though problems don't exist. But there is a day coming (we're in the edge of it right now) when we'll see and know these things as we ought. We'll not have to go out in the world to the unsaved for help. People in the church shouldn't go to unsaved marriage counselors for help. There's help in God.

Chapter 2
How To Deal With Evil Spirits

We have found from the portions of Scripture referred to in Volume One that Satan was, in the beginning, a covering cherub, but that he and his angels are now fallen beings. We found also that these beings seek embodiment in man.

We read how an unclean spirit tries to go back into the same man it has come out of (Matt. 12:43-45). Let's not give the devil any more room to move in. We also have the record concerning the madman of Gadara who had a legion of demons in him.

Some time ago I was watching a television newscast in one of our larger cities. A medical doctor was being interviewed while he was visiting a scientific convention in that city. During the course of the interview the reporter mentioned the strides that had been made in medicine.

The doctor smiled and said the greatest thing they'd done was to prove Jesus Christ was a fake. This seemed to "jar" the reporter.

The doctor went on to explain what he meant. He said they had exploded the idea that there is such a thing as a demon having something to do with sickness. He said, in fact, that there is no such thing as a devil or demon.

That man was motivated by a demon and didn't realize it. He was in darkness. There *is* a spirit world, and that world is even more real than this physical world. Out there in that spirit world, there is God. Out there in that spirit world, there is the devil. Out there in that spirit world, there are angels and demons. We have to deal with them in our earth walk.

In Ephesians 6:12 Paul said, *"We wrestle not against flesh and blood."* When we can recognize our enemies, we will be equipped to meet them; but if we don't know about them, we can unconsciously open the door to the devil.

Evil spirits not only seek embodiment in man, they seek to oppress man with sickness and disease. We saw that Peter called sickness and disease satanic oppression in Acts 10:38. We have a record in the Gospels that Jesus dealt with Satan and demons when dealing with disease. The woman who came into the synagogue had a spirit of infirmity. (Whether or not there is an actual presence of a demon oppressing a body physically in sickness and disease, you can be sure the devil is behind the whole thing.)

The Word of God tells us that when Satan is finally barred from human contact, there will be nothing that will hurt or destroy (Rev. 21:4). But we can exercise authority over the devil and over sickness and disease today in the Name of Jesus.

Someone asked me, "If the devil is behind sickness, why is it that some conditions will respond to medical science and can be helped? Can you treat the devil with medicine?" The devil lies back of everything that hurts or destroys. Men have learned through experimentation that certain things exercise authority over others. Penicillin, for instance, will exercise authority over certain germs. But the Name of Jesus exercises authority over everything!

Wigglesworth's Deliverance

Smith Wigglesworth said that when he first received a gleam of light on the subject of divine healing, he and his wife decided they would go all out. They would trust God until they died. They wouldn't take any kind of medicine or see a doctor. That may sound extreme to some, but that was their conviction.

A short time later, Wigglesworth fell in the pulpit, doubled up with appendicitis. He was taken home, and people prayed all night with him. When morning came, he was worn out from the pain and suffering. He told his wife he believed this was his home call. He finally had a doctor examine him so an inquest wouldn't be needed. The doctor said Wigglesworth's appendix had burst and poison had spread throughout his system. There were no miracle drugs for it.

He said Wigglesworth would die whether he underwent an operation or not. The operation would only cause him to die more easily. Wigglesworth said he wasn't going to submit to an operation. He would just die.

Finally the doctor left. Wigglesworth was in a semiconscious condition and would drift away now and then. His wife was downstairs attending to the plumbing business. He heard the door open, and looking up, he saw an elderly lady about 82, and a boy who was 14 years old. He knew this woman considered anything that attacked the physical body to be of the devil. He said he would have argued until doomsday about having a devil in him, but they didn't wait for any argument.

The boy jumped up on the bed, dug his fist into Wigglesworth's side, and demanded the devil to come out in the Name of Jesus. Instantly Wigglesworth was all right. He said he got up and dressed, went downstairs, asked his wife if there were any orders in, and went out to do some plumbing.

When the doctor came back, Polly Wigglesworth ran to him and told him her husband was out on a job. The doctor remarked that Wigglesworth "would be brought back a corpse." In his meetings, Wigglesworth used to say that he was that corpse.

He said after that, he prayed for people with appendicitis on every continent of the earth. He always would dig his fist into their side and command the devil to come out in the Name of Jesus. He said he'd never had a case yet in which a person wasn't up and dressed in 15 minutes. You can't argue with success!

A Full Gospel minister once told me that this couldn't be true. He said if a spirit were causing sickness, how could you cut a spirit out of a person? He noted that people can be operated on for appendicitis and afterwards they're all right. So he said that couldn't be the devil, because you can't cut the devil out of a person.

This makes me think of a preacher who told on the radio about a church member whose husband was a scoundrel. The man would come home drunk and beat her up. She kept requesting prayer for him. One time she came in to talk to this minister. He told her she should just knock the "hell" out of him with a ball bat when he came in like that. But you can't *knock* the devil out of people.

You can't *cut* a spirit out of a person either. Yet, if a certain part of the body were affected by a spirit, then naturally, when that part was cut out there wouldn't be anything for the spirit to affect. It isn't a matter of cutting out the devil — that ought to be plain enough.

Use Your Authority

These spirits do oppress people, whatever kind of spirits they are — that is how they operate.

There are degrees of demonic *oppression.* Sometimes a person is more oppressed than he is at other times. There also are degrees of *possession* — a person can be more or less possessed.

But, thank God, we're the ones who have authority in this life. We can determine, by taking advantage of what belongs to us, to be overcomers, controlled by the Spirit.

I will never forget when the Lord appeared to me in a vision in 1952 in the state of Oklahoma. He said, "I'm going to talk to you about the devil, demons, and demon possession."

This experience lasted about an hour and a half. Jesus stood before me as I knelt. Suddenly an evil spirit that looked like a monkey jumped up between us and caused a black cloud to appear. I couldn't see Jesus, but I could hear Him. He kept right on talking. Meanwhile, the spirit threw his arms and legs out and hollered in a shrill voice, "Yakety-yak, yakety-yak, yakety-yak."

He kept on acting that way and thoughts ran through my mind faster than machine gun bullets could fire.

I thought, *Dear Lord! I'm missing what Jesus is saying* (instruction He was giving me about dealing with the devil). I heard the sound of His voice, but I couldn't distinguish the words because of this "yakety-yak" business. I couldn't see Jesus because the cloud was there.

Then I thought, *Doesn't Jesus know? Doesn't He know I'm not hearing Him? Why doesn't Jesus do something about it? Why does He allow it?*

Finally, in desperation, I spoke to the spirit. I said, "I command you to shut up in the Name of Jesus!"

When I said that, he hit the floor like a sack of salt: "kerplop." The dark cloud disappeared, and I could see Jesus. Then Jesus said something that absolutely astonished me — something that upended my theology. (We get so concerned about theology that we miss the Bible.)

Jesus pointed to that little fellow lying there (and not only lying there — he was shaking all over, trembling from head to foot and whining). Jesus said, "If you hadn't done something about that, I couldn't have."

Listen and reign! Let it slip by you and be in slavery!

In my astonishment, I said, "Lord! I know I misunderstood You. I'm sure I did. You didn't say you *couldn't*" — and I pointed to that little fellow still lying there whimpering and shaking all over — "You said You *wouldn't,* didn't You?"

Jesus said, "I said," — and He pointed to him — "if you hadn't done something about that, I *couldn't.*"

Now understand "that" didn't include just the demon; it included the dark cloud that shut off the vision of Jesus and heaven. It included communication that didn't get through — prayers, or whatever.

I said, "Lord, I know something happened to me. You didn't say You *couldn't;* You said You *wouldn't,* didn't You?"

And very emphatically He said, "No! I didn't say I *wouldn't;* I said I *couldn't.*"

"O dear Lord," I said. "I can't accept that. It's against everything I've ever believed! It's against everything I've ever preached!"

I said, "I won't accept any vision unless You can prove it to me from the Bible — particularly the New Testament. You said in Your Word, *'In the mouth of two or three witnesses every word may be established'* " (Matt. 18:16).

Do you think He got angry with me? No, He smiled so sweetly and said, "I'll go you one better; I'll give you four."

He said, "There's no place in the New Testament where the Church or Christian believers are told to pray against the devil. To pray against the devil is to waste your time."

When He said that to me I said, "Dear Lord! I've wasted so much time!"

He said, *"The New Testament tells believers themselves to do something about the devil. And if they don't, there won't be anything done. I've done all I'm ever going to do about the devil."*

That came as a real shock to me. "Now," He said, "I'll give you the four references which prove that. First of all, in Matthew 28, when I arose from the dead, I said, *'All power is given unto me in heaven and in earth'* (Matt.

28:18). The word 'power' means 'authority.' " (If you
stopped reading right there you'd say, "Why, dear Lord
Jesus, You do have authority here on the earth.")
But He said, "I immediately delegated my authority
on earth to the Church." In Mark 16 we are told to go into
all the world; *we're* authorized to do that.

> MARK 16:15-18
> 15 And he said unto them, Go ye into all the world, and
> preach the gospel to every creature.
> 16 He that believeth and is baptized shall be saved; but
> he that believeth not shall be damned.
> 17 And these signs shall follow them that believe; In my
> name shall they cast out devils; they shall speak with new
> tongues;
> 18 They shall take up serpents; and if they drink any
> deadly thing, it shall not hurt them; they shall lay hands
> on the sick, and they shall recover.

Jesus said to me, "Not one time does any New Testament writer tell you to pray to God or to Me, the Lord
Jesus Christ, to do anything about the devil. Every single
time they tell *you* to do it. *You're* the one who has
authority. *You're* the one who's to rule."
The next reference He gave me was James 4:7: *"Submit
yourselves therefore to God. Resist the devil, and he will
flee from you."*
Now, as Jesus said, you couldn't do that if you didn't
have authority over the devil. James is writing to believers.
This is not something to be foolish about. One preacher
told me he had the devil on the run. He said the trouble
was, *he* was running and the devil was after him.
James says to resist the devil and he will flee. I looked
up the word "flee" to get a clearer knowledge of it. One
shade of meaning was "to run from as if in terror." The
devil will run from you in terror. Most people are running
from him in terror. They're talking about what he's doing

and how he's keeping them sick and unsuccessful. They give the devil dominion over them. But let's talk about what God's Word says. Let's talk about the authority we have because of the Name of Jesus.

Sometimes people wonder why heaven seems unreal to them. (The devil is trying to blot it out.) They wonder why it seems they can't get through. (The devil is trying to cut heaven off.) They pray and wonder why God permitted a certain thing. (He has already said for you to do something about it.)

The fourth Scripture is Ephesians 4:27: *"Neither give place to the devil."* Jesus quoted that to me, saying, "That simply means, 'Don't let the devil have any place in you.'" He said, "That means the devil can't take any place in you unless you let him. That means you've got the authority."

Sometimes I'll put up with things when I know they ought not to be. Finally I'll put my foot down and tell the devil he's gone far enough. I tell him to stop.

God said in His Word for *you* to resist the devil. God is trying to get us to exercise what really belongs to us.

And although we don't have authority over human spirits, any Christian can take authority over the evil spirits *behind* such harassment. In the privacy of your own home, you can deal with the situation by saying, "You foul spirit that is operating through So-and-so (call their name), embarrassing, intimidating, hurting, deterring the ministry of this church, I command you to stop in Jesus' Name!"

Demons in the Church

One Pentecostal pastor who got some of my tapes on this subject said three men in his church had been causing him trouble. All three were born again and filled with the Holy Spirit, but anybody can yield to the devil. That doesn't mean you're unsaved because you yield to him. (If it did, there would be no one saved today!)

But sometimes, when something goes wrong in the church, people begin to operate in the natural, thinking, *Well, I don't like that,* or *The pastor is exercising too much authority.* And then the devil will bring other thoughts to their minds, and before long they're doing the devil's work, trying to undermine the pastor.

This was the case with the three men in this pastor's church. He had tried to deal with the problem by bringing it before the church board and talking to each of them individually. That only made it worse. Each of them had friends who were going to follow them, resulting in three divisions in the church. The pastor had almost despaired, thinking, *I believe I'll leave. I'm tired of fighting it.*

In the process of time, I had a chance to visit with this pastor. He said, "You know what I did? I listened to your tape, sitting there in my study. And I got up right in my study and said, 'You foul devil . . . Now I command you, spirit, that is operating through . . . .' and I called each of the three men's names, 'creating confusion and division in this church, I command you to stop, in the Name of Jesus.'" He said, "I just sat back down and said, 'Bless God, that settles it.'"

He said to me, "Brother Hagin, I want you to know that in ten days' time, this situation straightened out. In fact, those men became the greatest allies I had. The one who had caused the most trouble said, 'I don't know what in the world got into me. It seemed like some kind of influence came on me. But, thank God, it's gone. I want you to forgive me.'"

You see, some kind of influence had come upon him, and he had begun to think certain ways, and before he knew it, he had decided, "We need a new pastor; this one doesn't suit me." (The pastor wasn't supposed to suit him anyway. A pastor is supposed to suit the Lord!)

I'm well satisfied we have more authority than we have used. I believe the Spirit of God is saying we're about to come to a place where men will operate in the Spirit and see in the realm of the Spirit more than they have in the past. There will be great victories.

Now, I understand that the devil has power; he can do *some* things. That's not unscriptural. God led Israel out of Egypt, Aaron threw down his rod and the Pharaoh's magicians threw down their rods, and all of the rods became serpents (Exod. 7:11). Those magicians were of the occult. They matched miracle for miracle up to a point.

But here is something I like: Aaron's serpent swallowed up the rest of them! So don't be concerned with what the devil might do. We can swallow up his works in the Name of Jesus! Hallelujah!

Some years ago, I read about a Pentecostal woman missionary who was ministering in Africa during the '30s. She was left alone in the mission station for several days because of a shortage of workers.

During that time, the witch doctor of the village challenged her. He wanted to get rid of her. He told her, "I'll do a bigger miracle than you, and if I do, you must leave town — close the mission down and leave us alone. But if you do a bigger miracle than I do, we'll all follow your God."

She didn't know what to do. Actually, she didn't want to do anything, she was so afraid. She wished that the other missionary were there; he would know what to do. But the little flock who had been saved by their ministry encouraged her to accept the challenge, and she didn't want to let them down. She thought, *Lord, what am I going to do? What kind of miracle can I do?*

They met at the little mission church. The witch doctor placed himself flat on the floor, lying down, and entered into a state of meditation during the next 45 minutes. Suddenly he began to rise off the floor. He hung suspended in the air, as high as the pulpit, stretched out like a two-by-four plank where everybody could see him.

The woman missionary thought, *Dear God, how am I going to top that? What in the world am I going to do?* Suddenly the Spirit of God came upon her (when the anointing comes upon you, sometimes you'll act without thinking), and she ran up to the witch doctor, laid her hands on his head, and said, "Come out of him, devil, in the Name of Jesus!"

He hit the floor like a sack of salt, got up, ran down the aisle and out the door. You see, she swallowed up his miracle!

The witch doctor came back a week later and said, "I've lost my power. I can't do anything anymore." He wound up getting saved and filled with the Holy Spirit!

Our thinking is too small. If we'll grow spiritually, we'll realize God can keep us. He wants people to grow spiritually so they can stand on their own two feet. He wants them to take their place in Christ, knowing the Name of Jesus belongs to them as much as it does to the preacher or evangelist.

We need to realize that in our everyday combat — on the job, at home, wherever we are — we're facing these spirits. We have a right to use the Name of Jesus wherever we are. We can put the devil on the run!